Healthy Plates

FRUITS

VALERIE BODDEN

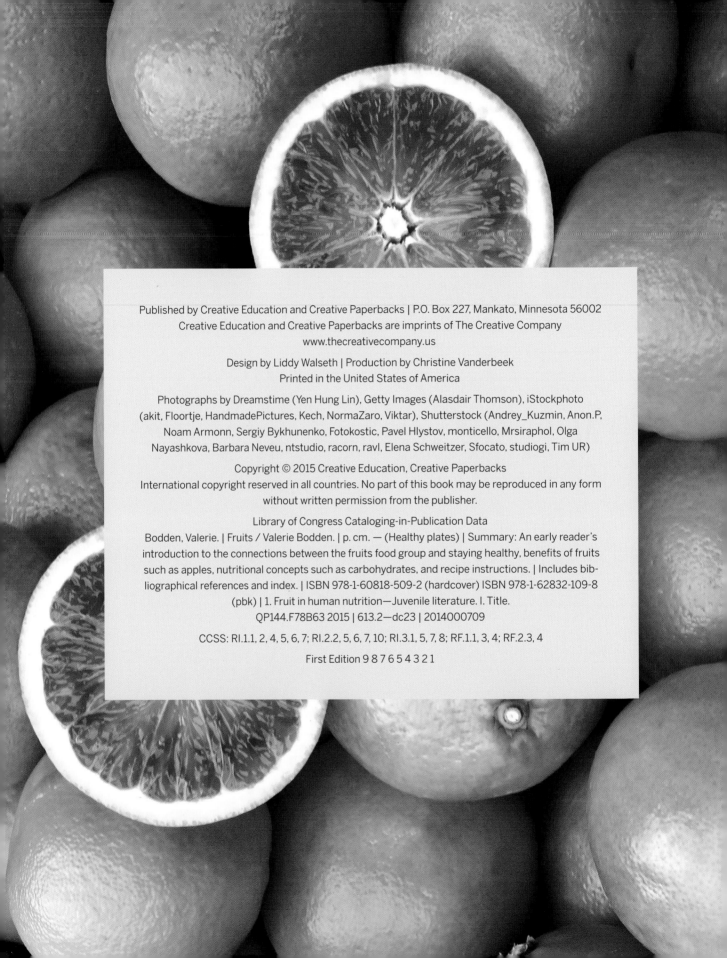

Published by Creative Education and Creative Paperbacks | P.O. Box 227, Mankato, Minnesota 56002
Creative Education and Creative Paperbacks are imprints of The Creative Company
www.thecreativecompany.us

Design by Liddy Walseth | Production by Christine Vanderbeek
Printed in the United States of America

Photographs by Dreamstime (Yen Hung Lin), Getty Images (Alasdair Thomson), iStockphoto (akit, Floortje, HandmadePictures, Kech, NormaZaro, Viktar), Shutterstock (Andrey_Kuzmin, Anon.P, Noam Armonn, Sergiy Bykhunenko, Fotokostic, Pavel Hlystov, monticello, Mrsiraphol, Olga Nayashkova, Barbara Neveu, ntstudio, racorn, ravl, Elena Schweitzer, Sfocato, studiogi, Tim UR)

Library of Congress Cataloging-in-Publication Data
Bodden, Valerie. | Fruits / Valerie Bodden. | p. cm. — (Healthy plates) | Summary: An early reader's introduction to the connections between the fruits food group and staying healthy, benefits of fruits such as apples, nutritional concepts such as carbohydrates, and recipe instructions. | Includes bibliographical references and index. | ISBN 978-1-60818-509-2 (hardcover) ISBN 978-1-62832-109-8 (pbk) | 1. Fruit in human nutrition—Juvenile literature. I. Title.
QP144.F78B63 2015 | 613.2—dc23 | 2014000709

CCSS: RI.1.1, 2, 4, 5, 6, 7; RI.2.2, 5, 6, 7, 10; RI.3.1, 5, 7, 8; RF.1.1, 3, 4; RF.2.3, 4

First Edition 9 8 7 6 5 4 3 2 1

TABLE OF CONTENTS

Growing Up

Your body needs food to give it energy and help it grow. But not all foods are good for you. Healthy foods contain the **nutrients** (*NOO-tree-unts*) your body needs to be at its best. Healthy foods are put into five food groups: dairy, fruits, **grains**, **proteins**, and vegetables. Your body needs foods from each food group every day.

Fruit Group

All fruits are part of the fruit food group. They can be fresh, frozen, or dried. Fruit juices are part of the fruit group, too.

FRUIT JUICE IS MADE BY SQUEEZING OR MASHING UP FRUITS.

Fruits have nutrients called carbohydrates (*kar-bo-HI-drates*). Carbohydrates give you energy to be active. They give your brain energy to think, too!

RUNNERS OFTEN EAT FOODS WITH CARBOHY-DRATES BEFORE A RACE.

Vitamins and Nutrients

Fruits have many **vitamins**. Fruits like oranges, kiwis, and berries have Vitamin C. Vitamin C helps your body fight sicknesses and heal cuts. Your body gets Vitamin A from watermelons, apricots, and other orange fruits. This vitamin helps your eyesight.

ONE CUP (237 ML) OF STRAWBERRIES HAS MORE VITAMIN C THAN AN ORANGE.

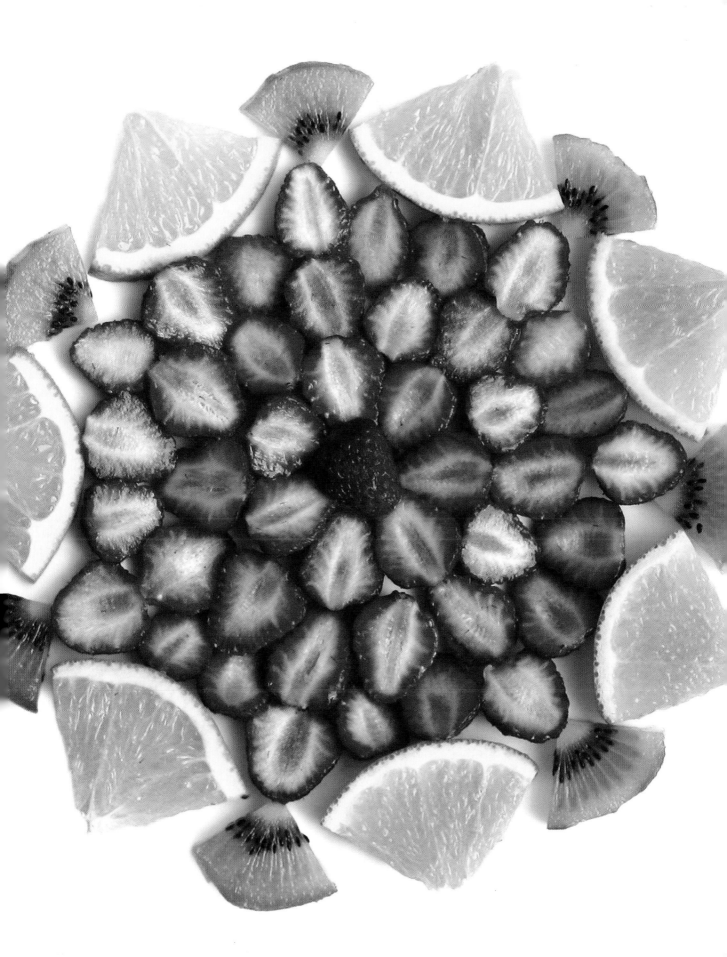

Fruits also have fiber. Fiber helps keep your **digestive system** healthy. Apples, pears, and bananas have lots of fiber. Fiber is found in the skins and **pulp** of most fruits. These parts are not used in juice, so juice does not have much fiber.

THE FIBER FOUND IN APPLES CAN KEEP YOUR BLOOD HEALTHY, TOO.

Some fruits also have potassium.
Potassium is a nutrient that
helps keep your heart healthy
by lowering **blood pressure**.
Bananas, prunes, and dried
peaches have lots of potassium.

PRUNES ARE MADE
FROM PLUMS (RIGHT).
THEY ARE THE DRIED
FORM OF THE FRUIT.

How Much?

Most kids should eat about 1 to 1.5 cups (237–355 ml) of fruit each day. One small apple counts as a cup of fruit. So does a large banana, orange, or peach. About 32 grapes or 8 large strawberries make up a cup. People who are older or more active can eat more fruit.

Healthy Living

It is easy to eat plenty of fruits. Put berries on top of your cereal or pancakes. Have a fruit salad with lunch. Try a baked apple for dessert.

PLAYING SOCCER IS A
GOOD WAY TO RUN AND
GET SOME EXERCISE!

Eating fruits is part of being healthy. Exercising is another part. Try to move your body an hour every day. Exercising and eating healthy can be fun—and can make you feel good, too!

MAKE A FRUIT SNACK:

FRUIT BOAT

1 BANANA
4 STRAWBERRIES
1 HANDFUL BLUEBERRIES
2 TBSP. PEANUT BUTTER

Ask a grown-up to help you cut the banana in half the long way. Spread peanut butter on the cut sides of the banana pieces. Top your banana "boats" with strawberries and blueberries, or add other favorite fruits. Enjoy your healthy fruit snack!

GLOSSARY

blood pressure—how hard a person's blood pushes against the blood vessels, or tubes that carry blood through the body

digestive system—the parts of your body used in breaking down food and getting rid of waste

grains—parts of some kinds of grasses, such as wheat or oats, that are used to make bread and other foods

nutrients—the parts of food that your body uses to make energy, grow, and stay healthy

proteins—foods such as meat and nuts that contain the nutrient protein, which helps the body grow

pulp—the soft inside part of a fruit

vitamins—nutrients found in foods that are needed to keep your body healthy and working well

READ MORE

Head, Honor. *Healthy Eating*. Mankato, Minn.: Sea-to-Sea, 2013.

Kalz, Jill. *Fruits*. North Mankato, Minn.: Smart Apple Media, 2004.

Llewellyn, Claire. *Healthy Eating*. Laguna Hills, Calif.: QEB, 2006.

WEBSITES

My Plate Kids' Place
http://www.choosemyplate.gov/kids/index.html
Check out games, activities, and recipes about eating healthy.

PBS Kids: Healthy Eating Games
http://pbskids.org/games/healthyeating.html
Play games that help you learn about healthy foods.

Note: Every effort has been made to ensure that the websites listed above are suitable for children, that they have educational value, and that they contain no inappropriate material. However, because of the nature of the Internet, it is impossible to guarantee that these sites will remain active indefinitely or that their contents will not be altered.

INDEX